tECHiES™

Larry Ellison

Larry Ellison

{ Sheer Nerve }

DANIEL EHRENHAFT

TWENTY-FIRST CENTURY BOOKS
BROOKFIELD, CONNECTICUT

Special thanks to Bradley Wellington for contributing "Tech Talk"

Design by Lynne Amft

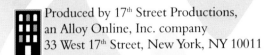
Produced by 17th Street Productions,
an Alloy Online, Inc. company
33 West 17th Street, New York, NY 10011

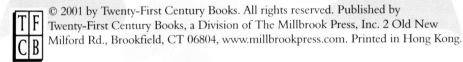
Library of Congress Cataloging-in-Publication Data
Sherman, Josepha.
    Larry Ellison : sheer nerve / by Josepha Sherman.
        p. cm. — (Techies)
    ISBN 0-7613-1962-X (lib. bdg.)
    1. Ellison, Larry—Juvenile literature. 2. Computer software industry—United States—
Juvenile literature. 3. Businessmen—United States—Biography—Juvenile literature. [1.
Ellison, Larry. 2. Businesspeople. 3. Computer software industry—Biography. 4.
Oracle Corporation—History.] I. Title. II. Series.

HD9696.63.U62 S53 2001
338.7'610053'0973—dc21

                                                                        2001027167

contents

Introduction

The Man, the Myth...

When you picture somebody who revolutionizes software, you might think of a skinny guy in ill-fitting pants and horn-rimmed glasses who spends all day hunched over a keyboard. Or one of those twenty-year-old technowizards who create new ways to download music off the Internet. Or maybe you think of a tattooed cybervillain who gets his kicks writing viruses.

But chances are you do *not* think of Larry Ellison.

That is because fifty-six-year-old Larry Ellison is the outrageous exception to every rule of the software industry. Slick and wild, he is equally as famous for being founder and chairman of the multibillion-dollar Oracle Corporation as he is for just being himself. Everybody in Silicon Valley knows Larry.

He is the crazy character who spends as much time in the cockpit of one of his many stunt planes as he does in the boardroom.

While most computer entrepreneurs are camera-shy, Ellison craves attention. While most are soft-spoken and polite, he talks loudly and uses a lot of four-letter words. Microsoft chairman Bill Gates tends to wear rumpled khakis; Larry Ellison prefers four-thousand-dollar suits. He has been

Larry Ellison: computer entrepreneur and Silicon Valley's "clown prince"

married and divorced three times. He has a unique gift for shocking, offending, and charming people—all at once. As journalist David Kaplan wrote, he is Silicon Valley's "clown prince."

Yet he is also full of surprising contradictions. Behind the outgoing facade lies a deeply private individual, one whom few others (even his three former wives) say they know well. And for all his public shenanigans, Ellison spends a great deal of time alone—reading, flying, meditating . . . and, some say, plotting his next big corporate move. He can be extremely generous and, at turns, quite greedy. According to one rumor, he signs all his checks in green ink because green is the color of money ("Ridiculous," he scoffs, "I just like the color"), and while he can speak intelligently about almost any topic imaginable—from ancient Japanese art to zoology—he often makes glaring mistakes about the details of his own life.

As a matter of fact, Ellison has been accused many times of being . . . well, somewhat less than honest. "Does Larry lie?" asks a smiling colleague who has known him for thirty years.

"We prefer to say Larry has a problem with tenses. For instance, 'our product is available now' might mean that it'll be available in a few months or that Larry was thinking about maybe one day developing the product."

And what exactly *is* the product? Many people have been asking that same question for years. For such a huge corporation, Oracle is pretty mysterious. You may have heard their commercial: "Software powers the Internet. Ninety-six percent of all Internet companies use Oracle software."

That may be true, but it still does not really explain what Oracle does. Ellison is perfectly happy to keep people guessing, though. It is enough for people to know that if they surf the web, they are probably using Oracle software. Oracle enables a person to find a zip code in Alabama, or a recipe for apple pie, or the cheapest airfare from Zurich to Zimbabwe. In other words, Oracle can do almost anything. Or so Ellison claims. And *that* is enough to keep people investing in the company—which in turn keeps Ellison's bank account filled with billions of dollars.

Of course, Ellison's wild words and so-called "problem with tenses" have made him a lot of powerful enemies. But his colorful persona has won over more than a fair share of friends as well. After all, who else can brag about hanging out regularly with such diverse celebrities as Apple Computer founder Steve Jobs, legendary NFL quarterback Joe Montana, and President Bill Clinton? It is all the more surprising when you consider that Larry Ellison is one of the few American billionaires (yes, *billionaires*) who did not even graduate from college.

"Someone once accused me of being unnecessarily interesting," he boasted a few years ago. And that pretty much says it all. He may not be known for his modesty, but one thing is certain: Larry Ellison is never, ever dull.

CHAPTER ONE

The Kid with Something to Prove

A Hard Road

LIKE MANY ENTREPRENEURS, LAWRENCE JOSEPH ELLISON DID NOT START OUT A RICH KID. FAR FROM IT. HE WAS BORN ON AUGUST 17, 1944, ON THE LOWER EAST SIDE OF MANHATTAN. AT THE TIME IT WAS A POOR AND CROWDED NEIGHBORHOOD MADE UP LARGELY OF EASTERN EUROPEAN IMMIGRANTS. HIS MOTHER, FLORENCE, WAS ONLY NINETEEN. SHE WAS NOT MARRIED. ELLISON NEVER EVEN KNEW HIS REAL FATHER.

WHEN HE WAS JUST NINE MONTHS OLD, ELLISON CAME

down with a severe case of pneumonia. Florence realized that she simply could not care for him. She had to work long hours, and she barely made enough to support herself. If her baby got sick again, there was a good chance he would die. So she sent little Larry

Larry's childhood home, Chicago, Illinois

up to Chicago to live with her aunt and uncle, Louis and Lillian Ellison, who lived in a relatively affluent neighborhood on the North Side of the city.

Larry Ellison did not learn that he was adopted until the age of twelve. He always just assumed that Louis and Lillian were his real parents. Learning the truth was difficult, "a tender subject," as he said later. It did not help either that his adoptive father was not very supportive of him. Apparently Louis Ellison told Larry repeatedly that "he wouldn't amount to anything." But Larry dealt with his pain and insecurity by vowing to make something of himself—to succeed in life, whatever it took.

He also developed a fierce independence, as first evidenced at the age of thirteen by his refusal to have a bar mitzvah. His father was enraged. The family was devoutly Jewish. All of Louis Ellison's children by a previous marriage had studied for and completed the ceremony. Who was Larry to refuse? But Larry simply was not a religious person. He figured: Why put on an act just to please his father?

The two would quarrel incessantly over this and many other issues. Ellison admits that he was much closer to his mother. Still, he claims he does not harbor any bitterness toward Louis

Ellison. "I think my dad had a wonderful effect on me," he says. "If fire doesn't destroy you, you're tempered by it."

Details of the rest of Ellison's teenage years are sketchy. When he was fifteen, his family moved from the North Side of Chicago to the South Side. Ellison would go on to describe the new neighborhood as "poor and tough." In fact, it was not much different from his old neighborhood, although it would develop a rough reputation in the years to come. His half sister Doris recently joked that every time she reads an article about her younger brother, the south side of Chicago gets worse and worse.

This kind of exaggeration is typical of the way Ellison talks about his life—meaning that if the plain truth is boring, he might as well stretch it a little. His oldest friends cannot seem to remember the specifics of his childhood, but they all agree on two points: He loved to tell stories, and all his best stories inevitably revolved around himself. Yet at the same time he was always funny, always positive, and never cruel. In some ways he simply saw the world as he wanted to see it, as "Larryland." What was the harm in that? His friend Rick Rosenfield put it this way: "Larry didn't fabricate. Larry just believed in everything he said."

A Rebel at Heart

When Ellison graduated from high school in 1962, he enrolled at the University of Illinois at Champaign-Urbana. He showed up on a cheap three-wheel Harley-Davidson motorcycle he had bought at a police auction, hoping to cultivate a rebel image. Unfortunately, Champaign-Urbana was not too interested in rebels. Ellison did not make many friends. College life was not nearly as exciting as he had expected. He tended to skip classes, preferring to read and study on his own. It was not long before he began to wish that he had gone somewhere else . . . such as California, maybe, where a rebellious youth movement was beginning to emerge.

After two fairly uneventful years Ellison's life was suddenly rocked by tragedy. His adoptive mother was diagnosed with cancer. She died on the first day of finals during his sopho-more year. Devastated, Ellison decided that there was no point in hanging around Illinois any longer. He did not even bother taking his final exams. Instead, he took off on his motorcycle and headed out west—to Berkeley, California.

The spirit of youthful independence out in the Bay Area was even greater than he had imagined. The kids out there were not at all like his friends back home. They had long hair and wild ideas. And they were not content to follow in their parents' footsteps. They wanted to change society—to make their own rules, to live a life free of prejudice and conformity. Ellison fell in love with Berkeley. He vowed to return after getting his college degree.

For the time being, however, he decided to return to the Midwest. He wanted to be close to his father, to keep him com-pany in Lillian's absence. At the end of the summer Ellison enrolled at the University of Chicago. As far as he was con-cerned, his new school was a big improvement from the University of Illinois, "a much more intellectual culture . . . and much more accepting of diversity." It was as close to California as he could get back east.

For a while he thought about becoming a doctor. The idea was short-lived, but the courses in science and medicine came in handy. They provided him with a lot of great material for his outlandish stories and stunts. Ellison understood that knowledge was power—particularly if it attracted attention and impressed people.

Here is a famous example. Once Ellison was pulled over for speeding while he and a friend were on a double date. When the police officer started to write him a ticket, Ellison made up an elaborate excuse on the spot—claiming that he was a resident at the University of Chicago Medical Center and that he was rushing to the hospital to assist in a "craniotomy." He was so convincing that the officer let him go without even so much as a warning.

To this day, his friends are not troubled by Ellison's lie; they are more impressed by how clever he was. It is classic Larry Ellison. Through charm, knowledge, and ingenuity he was able to talk his way out of a jam—and to get people to overlook the fact that he was not telling the whole truth.

Unfortunately, however, he was not able to charm his way through the rest of college. While Ellison was a whiz at science and mathematics, he had difficulty with languages. The University of Chicago requires that its students master at least one language before they graduate. Ellison took a

Ellison's beloved Berkeley, California

couple of courses in French but did poorly. He would later joke that he saw no reason to make his life miserable over learning French. After all, he knew enough to "understand what was on the menu [at a French restaurant]"—and that was what was most important to him. He ended up dropping out of college before exams.

But before he left the University of Chicago for good, he picked up a skill that would change his life forever. It was computer programming. Of course, he did not realize its importance at the time. A couple of friends had simply introduced him to the possibility of writing code for the big university mainframes as an easy way to make some extra money.

Ellison saw programming as a last resort—meaning that if he did not come up with a scheme that could make him a millionaire overnight, he at least had a skill that could pay the rent for the time being. He had no doubt that he *would* become a millionaire, though. Above everything else, he had unwavering confidence in himself. He just needed to figure out how he was going to make his fortune. That was the tricky part. The rest was easy.

It was the summer of 1966. Ellison was twenty-two years old. His father told him that he was worthless, a failure for having dropped out. But Ellison was driven to prove his father wrong. He was going to accomplish something on a massive scale—the kind of scale that would leave everyone back in Chicago gasping. So he decided to return to Berkeley, California, the land of his dreams. He never looked back.

CHAPTER TWO

Big Dreams, Big Database

Making the Most of His Time

WHEN LARRY ELLISON ROLLED INTO TOWN THAT SUMMER IN HIS AQUA-BLUE FORD THUNDERBIRD, HE HAD GOOD LOOKS, CHARM, INTELLIGENCE . . . BUT LITTLE ELSE. FLAT BROKE, HE WENT TO A BERKELEY EMPLOYMENT AGENCY FOR HELP IN FINDING A JOB. THE EMPLOYMENT AGENCY FOUND HIM SO APPEALING THAT THEY DECIDED TO HIRE HIM—AS A JOB COUNSELOR. ELLISON WAS DELIGHTED. AND IT WAS THERE THAT HE MET THE WOMAN WHO WOULD EVENTUALLY BECOME HIS FIRST WIFE. HER NAME WAS ADDA QUINN.

Like many other people, Quinn was instantly attracted to Ellison. She found him utterly irresistible. Sure, he had a short attention span. He would lose interest in a topic "in about three seconds"—as soon as he had learned everything about it. He also had no money. Apparently he lived on dime packages of Kraft macaroni and cheese. But none of that mattered to Quinn. "I hardly knew him," she would say later. "I agreed to marry him because he was the most fascinating man I'd ever met in my life. I knew I'd never be bored."

The couple were wed on January 23, 1967. Not one member of Ellison's family attended the ceremony. Ellison did not invite any of his old friends from back home either. A lot of people were offended. But Ellison wanted to keep his past at a safe distance until he felt he had truly made something of himself.

Soon after the wedding Ellison left the employment agency. Over the next few years he took various programming jobs at a number of large corporations. For the most part, he handled IBM mainframes. The work consisted of writing code, backing up data on other computers, and stringing the huge reels of magnetic memory tape. Hardly any of the computers of the late sixties and early seventies used disk operating systems, so everything was saved on tape, like a cassette player.

Generally the jobs were not very challenging. Ellison spent a lot of time reading, educating himself . . . and dreaming. He longed for more excitement. Most of all, he longed for more money. Programming paid well, but it did not make him rich.

Of course, that did not stop him from spending. He bought a house. He bought a thousand-dollar bicycle. He bought two sailboats. He treated himself to expensive meals at fancy restaurants; he even flew to Los Angeles to get a nose job from an exclusive Beverly Hills plastic surgeon. He figured there was no reason to save what he earned. It was only a matter of time before he would make it big.

His wife was not so sure, though. For seven years she watched as Ellison bounced restlessly from job to job. She became increasingly annoyed. He never settled down. And even though they often struggled to pay the bills, Ellison did not seem to care at all about how much money they had. He

Yosemite National Park, one of Larry's favorite vacation spots

preferred not to worry. About *anything.* "He had champagne tastes on a beer budget," she would later joke.

But Ellison believes that Adda Quinn simply lacked a greater vision. "She had a program, you know?" he says now. "Get promoted, have an ambition . . . and I was perfectly happy to do a little writing, play the guitar. I adored going to

Yosemite [National Park]. I valued my time more than the pursuit of money."

That last part is probably an exaggeration. Larry Ellison was *obsessed* with money—which is why he loved to spend it so much. But his apparent laziness was deceiving. In some respects, he was making the most of his time. He was weighing his options, learning as much as he could about the world before he committed to any one profession or venture.

Quinn, however, thought he was just fooling himself. She was certain that his easygoing, self-indulgent lifestyle would result in failure. By 1974 she simply became too fed up with all of his spending and floundering. She filed for divorce.

At first Ellison was heartbroken. He promised her that if she stayed with him, he would become a millionaire. She could have anything she wanted.

Needless to say, she did not believe a word of it. In fact, she pitied him for being so childish and unrealistic. Yet she still felt affection for him—in large part because she never stopped being fascinated by him. Who else would dare to promise such wealth with nothing but a vague dream of glory to back it up?

After time, even after a painful breakup, Larry Ellison and Adda Quinn remained friends. And when he *did* achieve success, he was very generous to her. He bought her parents a house; he gave her a car; he even gave her second husband a job. It was his way of making amends for the grief he had caused her during their marriage. But it was also his way of proving to her that he was right. He *had* become a millionaire. More than a thousand times over!

Right Place, Right Time

In 1974, however, the future did not look so bright for Ellison. He was almost thirty years old, divorced, and virtually penniless. To make matters even worse, he had just been fired from his most recent job—as a programmer for the Amdahl Corporation, a small mainframe computer manufacturer that no longer exists.

Ellison had been hired by Amdahl to write code. But he did not do much work. Instead he just sat around and talked. A lot. In fact, most people say that he hardly ever shut up. He talked about anything and everything—books, religion, art, politics, himself (anything except work, it seemed)—to anyone who would listen.

Luckily, one of the few people who *did* listen was an unassuming young programmer named Stuart Feigin. The two became fast friends. Feigin was amused and dazzled by Ellison's overwhelming personality. Like Adda Quinn and countless others, Feigin also says he found Ellison to be "irresistible"—although he could never say exactly why. Ellison just had that effect on certain people. Some hated him. Others were enthralled.

When Ellison was fired, he promised Feigin that he would start a new company and make them both rich. Feigin was extremely dubious. "Here was a guy who couldn't show up to lunch on time," he said. "How could he run a company?" Still, the two kept in touch after Ellison's departure. The friendship would eventually prove to be a stroke of good fortune for Ellison, as Feigin would later become one of Oracle's key players.

Ellison soon had another lucky break. He landed a new programming job—this time at Ampex, an audio and visual equipment company in Sunnyvale, California. There he met two more people who would play pivotal roles in his rise to fame and fortune.

The first was his boss, Bob Miner. As author Mike Wilson phrased it, Miner was the "anti-Larry." He was humble, quiet, and very careful with his money. The second man was a programmer named Ed Oates. Coincidentally, Oates had gone to high school with Adda Quinn. The two had been biology lab partners.

Like Miner, Oates was warm and thoughtful. He was also a genius when it came to computers, having worked for IBM's research and development department before coming to Ampex. And he was captivated by Larry Ellison.

Together these three men would form a company that would change the computer industry forever.

Code Name: Oracle

When Ellison came to Ampex, he was assigned work on a project that was being funded by the CIA. It was code-named "Oracle." As you might have guessed, Ellison liked the name so much that he eventually took it for his own company. And it was definitely a fitting name for the project. Oracles were prophets in ancient Greece. They supposedly had access to the infinite wisdom of the gods. The goal of Project Oracle was to create a vast database—a seemingly magical system that could access infinite amounts of information.

At the time, creating such a database seemed almost impossible. The hardware simply did not exist. Disk drives were in the early development stages, but they did not have much memory. Thousands of disks would be needed to create the database that the CIA wanted. The alternative was magnetic tape, which had more storage capacity—but *finding* a specific bit of data in its memory was difficult. A person had to scan through miles of tape. The CIA was looking for something small and fast.

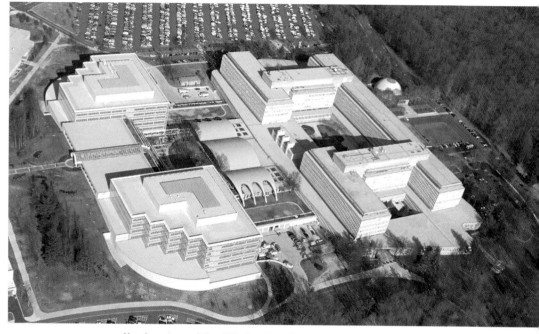
Headquarters of the CIA, Oracle's first customer

Ampex believed they had the solution. They were working on a way to store a "terabit" (a *trillion* bits) of data by using video-tape. Unlike regular magnetic tape, videotape could be scanned much faster. Plus it did not take up much space.

But the system never really worked. A big part of the prob-lem was that Ellison, Oates, Miner, and others had to write new software from scratch. Up until this point all databases used either hierarchical or network software—including the terabit system.

Hierarchical means starting from the top and going to the bottom. To understand how a hierarchical database works, imagine walking into a grocery store to buy a cold soda. You would probably head straight for the refrigerator, knowing that this is where cold sodas are kept. It is common sense. But a hierarchical database does not have common sense. It would search the entire store, starting at the very front—picking through all the candy and potato chips and everything else—until it finally came to the refrigerator. And if the refrigerator happened to be in the back of the store . . . well, then buying a soda could take a very long time.

In other words, a hierarchical database cannot see the *relationship* between the refrigerator and the soda. It just sees a refrigerator as another storage space—not a place where sodas are specifically kept cold. So it does not know to skip over all the other shelves.

A *network* database can help solve this problem by linking certain kinds of information. But every link has to be programmed into the computer. Even a network database that connects two simple bits of information such as "soda" and "refrigerator" requires hundreds of lines of code.

The CIA wanted a database that could instantly connect and cross-reference data without having to be programmed on

Larry Ellison spreads the word about Oracle.

the spot. Therefore, the trick was to create a *relational* database: a database with software that could automatically understand the relationship between different kinds of information.

It was a bold idea. In theory, you would not have to be a programmer to use it. Instead of writing new code for each use, you would only have to plug in a few words. The software would take care of the rest. More important, the software could adapt according to your needs. Yes, it could tell you that cold soda was in the refrigerator. But it could also tell you *how* cold the soda was, the cost of each soda, the amount of calories per serving. . . .The possibilities were, quite literally, endless.

As it turned out, the idea for a relational database was not even brand-new. In fact, IBM had been talking about creating one for years. They just lacked the technology to do it.

The Good Old Days of Software

In the early 1970s, IBM was the undisputed leader of the computer industry. Everybody else followed its lead. But unlike many of the computer companies today, IBM did not try to keep its research and development a secret. This was particularly true when it came to software. Several members of IBM's research-and-development team had already written articles about the possibility of developing software for relational databases. These articles were available to the public.

The reason for the openness was simple: Software was not seen as a way to make money. It was not something you could *sell*. It was invisible. IBM and other high-tech companies made money by selling hardware, the stuff you could see—the keyboards, the screens, the blinking lights, the cool wires and gadgets. Computer stores back then did not even display software. Now when you walk into a computer store, you see boxes filled with programs or games or business applications. Back then you saw *computers*. And nothing else. That meant it was virtually impossible to add or change software—unless you were a programmer.

Every machine needed software, of course. But it was basically viewed as a kind of plumbing. Software was built right into a computer, in the same way that plumbing is built right into a house. You certainly would not want to buy a house *without* plumbing. On the other hand, you probably would not want to install it yourself either. Installation was up to the plumber himself—or in the case of computer software, the programmer.

In many ways the programmers for IBM and other companies *were* a lot like plumbers. They were all technicians with common skills and common goals. And they saw no reason to hide what they were doing from one another. There was no money at stake. They figured that any advancements they made on their own would benefit the entire industry. So they were constantly exchanging information. They were constantly thinking of new ways to write code, to improve memory—and, of course, to improve databases.

Stuart Feigin calls this era "the good old days of software." Other programmers agree—including Ed Oates, who took IBM's ideas about relational databases with him when he went to Ampex. And it is true: The dawn of the 1970s was a time of incredible excitement and camaraderie in the computer industry. Most programmers truly believed that they were united. They were all on the verge of creating a new society. Together they could change the world—in the same way that the Industrial Revolution had changed the world a century earlier.

In fact, it seemed the only programmer who was not caught up in the excitement and camaraderie was Larry Ellison.

Changing the Rules

Then again, Ellison had never been like other programmers. He might have been good at it (in typical fashion, he describes himself as "*really* good" at it), but programming had always just been a way to pay the bills. Anyway, he was not interested in making the world a better place through better software. He was interested in making money. For himself.

This made him different from other computer-industry titans who came before and after him. True, Bill Gates might have been driven by a similar desire to strike it rich—but he was also motivated by a dream of bringing a personal computer into every home in America. So was Steve Jobs. Marc Andreessen was motivated by a dream of making the Internet accessible to everyone. Larry Ellison was motivated by a dream of owning mansions and yachts.

Still, he *did* have something in common with these other successful entrepreneurs: He saw a hole in the marketplace. And he knew how he could fill it. Bill Gates and Steve Jobs were smart enough to see that lots of people would want personal computers. Larry Ellison was smart enough to see that lots of companies would want relational-database software. They would be willing to pay for it, too. After all, the CIA was willing to pay Ampex to help improve *its* database technology—and Ampex's terabit system did not even work.

Maybe it was luck; maybe it was intelligence . . . maybe it was just pure greed. But Ellison recognized that there was a huge future in relational data bases. Unfortunately, Ampex did not share his vision or urgency. Nobody else did either. Not even IBM. Sure, people at IBM were interested enough in the

Bill Gates: a tough competitor in the computer industry

technology to write papers about it. But they were still making plenty of money selling hierarchical databases. And if IBM was not working too hard to develop a new product, why should anyone else bother? IBM made the rules for the entire industry.

But Ellison wanted to make the rules, too. Or better yet, he wanted to *change* them. After all, he had always been a rebel at heart, ever since he had arrived in California in the summer of 1964. And at that time nothing in Silicon Valley was more rebellious than the idea of *selling* database software. Not only did it violate the principles of the programmers, who shared everything for free, but it also did not make sense to the big computer manufacturers, who preinstalled all the software themselves.

Of course, Ellison never cared about other people's principles. He thought of himself as a visionary. He wanted to be in charge. After a while he grew frustrated with taking orders at Ampex and decided to move on. He took a job as vice president of systems development at a computer company called Precision Instrument.

For the first time in his life, he was an executive. He loved it. He was finally in charge of something. Specifically, he was in charge of coordinating the manufacture of a machine called the PI 180. Huge and futuristic, the PI 180 was a database computer that relied on photographic memory—much like Ampex's failed terabit system.

There was only one problem. Precision Instrument did not have the software to make the PI 180 work. Nor did they have the programmers. Ellison was forced to look outside the company to find the people he needed. He figured that most programmers would ask for a few hundred thousand dollars to work on the project. But he was shocked to find that most asked for millions. Clearly this was a sign: Database programmers were in hot demand.

At that moment Larry Ellison suddenly came up with the plan that would change his life. He would start his *own* company, just as he had always dreamed of doing. Instead of hiring freelance programmers he would ask his old friends Miner and Oates to be his partners. Together they would put in a bid for the PI 180 project. They would ask for less money, so they would be sure to get the job. Then they would get to work on creating a functioning relational database. They would solve the problems that IBM and Ampex and Precision could not.

And they would all get very rich in the process.

Anything's Possible

To this day, Ellison claims that he did not have any grand plan of conquering the database market. He says he founded a new company simply because he wanted to be his own boss. He says he was not even sure what the new company would *do*— at least not after the PI 180 contract. Maybe they would do some consulting. Maybe they would invent a new product. Or maybe they would focus on research and development. . . .

In retrospect, it seems that Ellison might once again be stretching the truth just a little bit. For one thing, the timing for creating a relational database could not have been better. *Everybody* was looking to improve and enlarge their databases. And IBM was not doing anything about it. That meant that Ellison had virtually no competition.

Ellison also had the perfect partners. Oates and Miner had also been working on relational software. Sure, the software did not technically exist yet—but with Oates and Miner at the helm, it *would* exist. Ellison knew it. And as long as potential customers believed that it could exist (or if Ellison gave the impression that it *already* existed; wink, wink) . . . well, then he and his partners would be in business for a long time.

Miner went along with Ellison's idea to start a new company right away. He was looking for a change. The terabit memory project at Ampex clearly had no future. Oates, however, was a little more reluctant. What if their software did not work? Worse, what if nobody wanted to hire them after Precision Instrument? Then they would be unemployed. They would be the laughingstock of the industry.

But Ellison convinced Oates to thrust his doubts aside. They *had* to give this company a try. Oates simply had to trust him on this. Of the three, Ellison was by far the best businessman. Well, that was what he believed, anyway.

In the end, it was just too tough to argue with Ellison. He had a way of making anything seem possible. He also had a way of making himself look very smart. Oates gave in. And he would be very, very glad he did.

CHAPTER THREE

Oracle Is Born

Making Their Move

IN THE SUMMER OF 1977, PRECISION INSTRUMENT AWARDED THE PI 180 CONTRACT TO LARRY ELLISON, BOB MINER, AND ED OATES. THE THREESOME ASKED FOR $400,000 FOR THEIR SERVICES. THIS MARKED THE BIRTH OF THE COMPANY THAT WOULD LATER BECOME ORACLE.

MINER AND OATES QUIT THEIR OTHER JOBS IMMEDIATELY. BUT ELLISON STAYED AT PRECISION TO HELP COORDINATE THE PROJECT, WITH THE UNDERSTANDING THAT HE WOULD SOON LEAVE. FOR YEARS TO COME HE WOULD LOVE JOKING ABOUT this odd set of circumstances: He had founded Oracle, but he was not even its first employee.

In the weeks that followed, the three men kicked around various possible company names. Oates wanted something silly: "Nero Systems: We Fiddle While You Burn." This was a reference to the Roman emperor Nero—the lunatic who insisted on playing his violin while Rome burned to the ground. But eventually they decided that a silly name would be too risky. They settled on something very dry and to the point: Software Development Labs (SDL).

Before SDL officially got started, the three men had to take an important first step. They had to declare how much their new company was worth and then divide this worth into shares of stock. This way, in the future, they would be able to sell SDL's stock to the public if the company did well.

Ellison and the others figured that SDL was worth $2,000. It was a small amount, but SDL was a small company with only one customer. The three employees divided this number into one hundred thousand shares of stock at two cents each.

Ellison bought 60 percent of the stock for $1,200. The other two men split the rest of it at $400 apiece. Their hope, of course, was that the company's value would increase over time and that shares would eventually be worth a lot more than two cents.

As of this writing, Oracle is worth roughly $50 billion. It is safe to say that SDL's hope was well founded.

Later, many of Ellison's enemies would accuse him of being unnecessarily greedy for taking such a large percentage of SDL's stock. But Ellison laughed off the criticism. The company was his idea, so why should he not have the biggest piece of the pie? Besides, Oates and Miner agreed with him. "Larry was the prime mover behind this thing," Oates said. "There was no question that Larry was pushing this idea a lot harder than either Bob or I would have pushed it. He had more chutzpah . . . so he got the chutzpah bonus."

A Fresh Start

Clearly, Ellison was more excited than the other two about making a fresh start in his life. Coincidentally, 1977 also marked another fresh start for the thirty-two-year-old businessman. At the beginning of the year he married his second wife, a young woman named Nancy Wheeler.

The story of their meeting and marriage was classic Ellison. In late 1976 he had gone to talk to a couple (he claims he cannot remember their names now) about buying their used Mercedes. The wife kept going on about how she knew "the perfect girl" for Ellison. The husband said he was not sure, although he agreed that this girl—Nancy Wheeler—was "the best-looking girl [he had] ever seen in his life." That got Ellison's attention. The next day he called her. She was in fact good-looking—as well as funny and smart. A few months later he proposed to her. He says he also ended up buying the Mercedes.

Still, his new company was his first priority. SDL officially opened for business on August 1, 1977, renting office space in the Precision Instrument building in Santa Clara, California. Ellison immediately brought in another programmer—a fellow Ampex veteran named Bruce Scott, who was young and extremely talented. He was the very first person who ever wrote a line of code for SDL.

Scott is not likely to forget the first day he came to work for the new company. It was also his first real taste of Larry Ellison. Apparently, Scott was trying to hook up one of SDL's computers to the central terminal at Precision Instrument. But a wall stood in the way. Connecting the computers seemed impossible. He asked Ellison what he should do. Ellison replied by picking up a hammer and smashing a hole in the wall. Now Scott could hook up the computers, right?

This act was perfectly symbolic of the way Ellison handled business in the beginning months of SDL. If there was no easy solution to a problem, well, he would just have to create one— no matter what stood in his path. Any problem could be solved. Larry Ellison would simply worry about the consequences later.

Or not at all.

On to Something Big

Within a year SDL had finished its work for Precision Instrument. The project was a failure, although in all fairness, this was not SDL's fault. It had created excellent software. It just did not work on the PI 180. The machine was too old-fashioned. If the PI 180 had used floppy disks, the SDL software would have functioned perfectly. In tests it had worked well on other computers. But the PI 180 used rhodium-plated strips, which were too clunky, too full of bugs. As Mike Wilson put it: "The software talked, but the hardware didn't listen."

Precision was forced to agree. They ended up scrapping the PI 180 altogether.

Luckily SDL had already been paid—so failure did not affect the company at all. In fact, the members of SDL were in high spirits. They had used the money very wisely. While working for Precision, SDL had also been hard at work experimenting with relational-database software. Oates, Miner, and Scott had done the bulk of the programming, while Ellison scurried around Silicon Valley, stirring up interest in his company's work. A buzz was starting to grow: SDL was on to something big.

But this time Ellison was not stretching the truth. Much to SDL's collective surprise, the company really *was* on to something big.

The hard work paid off very suddenly, it seemed. Once again they owed a lot of credit to IBM, which had published another set of papers: "System R: Relational Approach to Database Management."

Ellison could not believe what he found in the papers. Neither could Oates. The collection was in essence an instruction manual on how to build relational software. For Ellison it was like finding a key to a bank vault filled with cash.

Oates did not waste any time. He got his hands on the System R papers, passed them along to Miner and Scott—and before he knew it, SDL found themselves with a working relational database. The software still had many problems, but it was definitely a first.

To this day, many people wonder: Why did IBM not make the most of its own technology? Why did IBM just give it away? Perhaps because it never suspected that a brash group of young programmers would swipe its idea and use it to make billions. Of course, SDL did not really steal from IBM. The System R papers *were* available to the public. But IBM was from the old school of programming: Advancements in software were to be shared, not sold. In this respect the programmers at IBM were very naive.

Ellison was not from *any* school—except his own. He saw the computer industry as a battleground, not a brotherhood. If SDL did not create and sell a relational database, somebody else would beat them to it. One company's loss or misstep was another company's profit. He hoped that the company to profit would be SDL. IBM was too shortsighted to realize its mistake in making its knowledge public, and Ellison knew he had to act quickly. He had no trouble convincing the others at SDL to do the same.

At first SDL's relational database worked only on Digital Equipment Corporation (DEC) minicomputers. But Ellison's goal was to create software that could be used on any computer. In that way SDL would basically have to write only one program—then copy it and sell it. Less work, more money.

Oates and the others agreed. They got to work immediately.

Ellison, not to be outdone, began dropping hints around Silicon Valley that the software already existed. He called it Oracle—after the CIA-funded project at Ampex. It was the "one-size-fits-all computer program." It could work in any environment. It was portable. Ellison liked to say it was "promiscuous" because it would get involved "with anybody."

Sure, he was exaggerating a little bit. But he saw no harm in getting a head start on selling a product that would surely be operational in a matter of weeks. After all, Oates and the others were among the best programmers in the business.

Promises, Promises

In order to draw more attention to his new company and their new product, Ellison moved from the Precision offices in Santa Clara to a suite in Menlo Park, the very heart of Silicon Valley. He and the others also decided that the name of their company was too vague. They dropped SDL and became Relational Software, Inc. (RSI)—so that people would know exactly what they were doing.

Almost immediately, in December 1978, RSI found their first customer for Oracle. Or rather, their first customer found *them*. It was the CIA.

Needless to say, the CIA was not pleased that Ellison had stolen the name of their project and used it for his own software. But their annoyance quickly faded when they saw what RSI's "Oracle" could do. It was truly the database of the future—fast, efficient, and user-friendly. The CIA asked for two versions—one for an IBM mainframe and the other for a DEC minicomputer called the VAX. Naval intelligence also came knocking on RSI's door. They wanted a version of Oracle to run on a Unix operating system.

Ellison was thrilled. Oates, Miner, and Scott, on the other hand, were nervous. RSI suddenly found themselves with two powerful customers, both of whom were asking for software that did not technically exist yet. In a mad scramble the three programmers began to adapt Oracle so it could deliver what Ellison had promised.

To help them out, Ellison contacted his old friend Stuart Feigin and offered him a job. Feigin could not believe it. Ellison had actually done what he had claimed he would do years ago: He had started his own company. Not only that, RSI appeared to be doing pretty well for a start-up. After a few phone conversations Feigin found himself swept up in Ellison's dream of cashing in on relational databases. He became employee number five at RSI.

After several weeks of hard work the programming team at RSI came up with a real, portable version of Oracle. It turned out to be easier than they had expected. They rewrote the software in a programming language called C—which could be understood by many different kinds of machines. Nobody had ever used C for database software before. And by using C in this way, RSI accomplished another first: They created corporate software that could be sold on a massive level. Almost any company could use it.

"[Making Oracle work] was forced upon us, really," Bob Miner would say later. "It was just a matter of necessity." And that was true. If RSI had not successfully created what Ellison had already sold, they would have been in big trouble. Yes, Ellison's business tactics might have been less than honest. Yes, they might have caused his colleagues a lot of stress. But one thing was certain: He got results.

These were exciting times for Larry Ellison. He had never been happier. He was making a living on his own terms. After the CIA and the navy, the customers came pouring in. RSI initially charged companies $48,000 per copy of Oracle. It was no small sum, but as Ellison had predicted, people were willing to spend it. He and his colleagues quickly made a lot of money. He was rich; he was his own boss; he was on the forefront of an exciting technology.

Best of all, people were starting to hear about him. He was becoming famous . . . at least within the small, closed world of Silicon Valley. And that was all that Larry Ellison had ever truly wanted—to be the center of attention (with the money to back up his ego, of course!).

Unfortunately, his personal life suffered. With all the deal making and running around, he barely had any time left to spend with his wife. Nancy Wheeler left him after only eighteen months of marriage. Like Adda Quinn, she saw Ellison as a hopeless case—a dreamer who was big on talk and had little to show for it.

But unlike Quinn, Nancy Wheeler felt no lasting affection for him. She thought he had no future. And as far as she could tell, this Oracle business did not have much of a future either. Ellison was bound to quit after a few years, just as he had quit school and every other job he had ever had. So as part of the divorce settlement, she sold her share of stock back to him for a measly five hundred dollars. Had she held on to it, it would have been worth several billion dollars today!

Once again, it seemed, Larry Ellison would have the last laugh.

CHAPTER FOUR

The Wild Life and High Times of a Billionaire

Oracle Systems Corporation

BY LATE 1982, RSI HAD GROWN FROM A COMPANY OF FIVE TO A COMPANY OF OVER THIRTY. IT WAS DOING $2.4 MILLION OF BUSINESS A YEAR AND GROWING RAPIDLY. ELLISON DECIDED TO CHANGE THE NAME AGAIN, FROM RSI TO ORACLE SYSTEMS CORPORATION.

IN THE EARLY 1980S TRENDY, CUTTING-EDGE COMPANIES OFTEN NAMED THEMSELVES AFTER THEIR MOST SUCCESSFUL PRODUCTS. AND IF ELLISON WAS ANYTHING, HE WAS TRENDY and cutting-edge. Yet on a more practical note, the new name helped distinguish Ellison's team from another new company, Relational Technology, Inc. (RTI). Over the next few years RTI would become Oracle's biggest competitor.

In spite of Ellison's progress and growing reputation as a deal maker, the road was not always smooth at Oracle. For starters, the software did not always work. The early versions had a tendency to erase data. Sometimes they produced incorrect information. Sometimes they simply crashed. Even the CIA's version of Oracle turned out to be full of bugs— although the agency did not seem to mind. According to one Oracle employee, a representative of the CIA told him: "We bought this thing knowing damn well it wasn't going to work. We were buying an idea."

Also, Ellison's "problem with tenses" continued. He sold software that had not been perfected or even invented: "vaporware," as it came to be known. Often Oracle shipped empty boxes of their products just to meet the deadlines in their contracts. When a customer would call to complain that his software was missing, the staff at Oracle would apologize and say that they had made a mistake. Then they would ship the box again. This "mistake" bought them a few extra days or weeks to finish working on what they had agreed to deliver.

Ellison might not have been entirely honest with his customers (although he will never admit it). His unique genius, however, lay in his ability to convince them that Oracle *did* work, that it *did* exist, and more important, that it was the best and most reliable database software on the market. He sold it as aggressively as he possibly could. It did not matter what the problems were or that the software might only be an idea in a programmer's head. What mattered was that people believed in it.

But Ellison's relentless pace and lofty claims made life extremely difficult for people at his company. Programmers often worked sixty or seventy hours a week, trying to solve problems before an irate customer called and demanded to know why Oracle's software had destroyed all of their data. Bruce Scott, among others, simply could not take the strain anymore. He quit the same year that RSI became Oracle. Later he said that Ellison told him: "I cannot run this business and tell the truth to customers. It's not possible." Ellison claims he has no memory of ever saying such a thing.

Stuart Feigin agrees that Ellison rubbed programmers the wrong way, although he is more forgiving than Scott. (Then again, Feigin is now worth over $100 million, thanks to his share of Oracle's stock.) "I was more interested in making software that I could be proud of," he says. "For Larry, the software only needed to be 'good enough.' The funny thing is that Larry thought I was the one who lacked ambition."

 Reasons to Celebrate

In 1983, Oracle's business doubled. Ellison's business strategy seemed to be working. But what exactly *was* his strategy? People at Oracle called it "GTM"—"Get the Money." That was pretty much it. Nothing else mattered. Ellison was interested in one thing: selling Oracle. Any way he could. Fortunately, people were buying it. The old Ellison charm was working.

Ellison had another reason to celebrate. His girlfriend at the time, Barbara Boothe, gave birth to his first child, a boy named David. On December 4 he married Boothe, and the three officially became a family. It seemed that Larry Ellison was finally beginning to settle down—at least when it came to his personal life.

Still, he was primarily devoted to his business. Oracle's sales doubled again in 1984. Unfortunately, though, Relational Technology, Inc., did better. Their sales tripled. For Ellison second place was not an option. He was too competitive. He always had to be the best. "It is not enough to succeed," he later told *The New York Times*. "Everyone else must fail."

That blunt statement perfectly sums up his ruthless philosophy. And he was not afraid to admit it. In that respect, anyway, he was much more honest about himself than a lot of other businesspeople.

Luckily, he got a break in edging RTI out of competition. And whom did he have to thank? IBM, of course—yet again. Oracle used a certain programming language, Structured Query Language (SQL), in developing their software. It was a language that Ellison, Oates, and Miner had lifted straight from IBM's System R papers.

In the early 1980s a committee was formed to set standards in relational-database technology so that companies would be able to communicate more easily with one another. The committee was made up of representatives from every top computer company as well as people in the government. It was a throwback to "the good old days of software," when programmers shared information for free.

But it also served a more practical purpose. Every single company used databases. And in order for their business to grow, they had to share and cross-reference information. Without some common features their databases would be totally isolated from one another's. No data could pass between them.

TECH TALK

What Is Oracle?

Oracle is the maker of the world's most popular (and, many would argue, most powerful) relational database. A database is a special program on a computer meant only for storing and retrieving data. The data are stored in what is generally referred to as a table. A table is like a chart stored by the computer. For example:

Name	Favorite Color
Bill	Blue
Brad	Red
Sue	Red

The above table keeps a list of people and their favorite colors. If we now wanted to make a web page that uses a database, we could use this table. Let us take the simple example of having page 1 ask your name and page 2 display your favorite color.

Goto database:	**found name**
Enter name:	**Bill**
Your favorite color is:	**Blue**

Now let us say you type in your name, and the database does not have it. We can add a third page that can ask you your favorite color. This will happen only one time.

Goto database: name not found
Enter name: Fred
What is your
favorite color?: Green

Once you have entered your favorite color, it is inserted into a new row in the table. Now the table looks like this:

Name	Favorite Color
Bill	Blue
Brad	Red
Sue	Red
Fred	Green

The next time you come to the site and type in your name, the site will remember your favorite color.

A database is what allows web pages to remember who you are, what time a plane takes off tomorrow, the stories in the newspaper, and anything else that you could ever want to remember.

The committee had two choices of languages: SQL or Query Language (QUEL), which was used by RTI. When IBM announced that it would make SQL the language for all its products, other companies followed its lead. It did not matter that QUEL was easier to use; IBM had spoken. The company still carried more clout than anyone else in the industry. In 1986 the committee officially declared that SQL would be the standard language for all databases. RTI never recovered. Through sheer luck Larry Ellison had come out on top.

Milestones

The year 1986 also marked several other important milestones in Ellison's life and career. On January 31, Barbara Boothe Ellison gave birth to their second child, Margaret Elizabeth. The parents nicknamed her Megan. Unfortunately, however, their joy would not last long. For months Ellison's wife had been feeling ignored and unappreciated, just as Adda Quinn and Nancy Wheeler had before her. The two fought, and their marriage ended that year in divorce.

Nevertheless, they remained friends. Barbara Ellison shared Adda Quinn's fascination and warmth for him. She even kept his name. And they still get together with the kids for holidays or even just to go out and have fun. Ellison continues to be extremely generous to his third former wife, as he is with Adda Quinn.

Now, of course, he has the means to be generous. But back in 1986 his financial security was not so certain . . . at least, not until March 12. Because on that day Oracle "went public" with their stock. People outside the company were finally able to buy shares of the company. Ellison still owned the majority of shares, but they did not have a clear value until he knew how much other people were willing to pay for them. And as it turned out, people were willing to pay even more than he had expected. At the end of the day he was officially worth $93 million. His dream of wealth had come true.

The Competition

As with many of his triumphs, though, the sweetness wore off quickly. The very next day, March 13, 1986, another computer entrepreneur went public with *his* company. The man's name was Bill Gates. The company was Microsoft. And at the end of *that* day Gates was worth more than $300 million!

Larry Ellison had been beaten. And he hated it. Thus began a long-standing competition between the two (or battle, depending on how you look at it) that continues to this day. While they are always cordial to each other in public, they love criticizing each other. And until very recently Gates always had the upper hand. His business had bigger profits. His face appeared on more magazine covers. Gates continues to make more headlines—although nowadays it is for his troubles rather than his successes. The U.S. government determined that Microsoft competed unfairly, and now Gates's giant has been split into three companies. For the first time ever it seems that Bill Gates's reign over the computer industry might be slipping. And Ellison is eager to step in.

But back in the late 1980s, Ellison was always number two to Gates's number one. So he dealt with his second-place status the only way he knew how: by showing off. He might not have been as rich or powerful as Gates, but he sure was not as boring either.

His first move was to build new headquarters for Oracle: six huge glass towers around an artificial lake in Redwood City. The buildings looked like something out of a science-fiction movie. They were certainly unlike the offices of any other computer company at the time. And while they were spectacular on the outside, they were even more impressive on the inside. There were $5,000 espresso machines, a gym, designer furniture. . . . Each tower even had its own gourmet restaurant. Ellison wanted to prove to the world that Oracle was different. Oracle had style. They were not just better than the other software companies; they were in an entirely different league.

The towering glass structures of Oracle headquarters

This is not to say that Oracle did not continue to experience bumps along the road. Occasionally, Ellison's shaky business practices caught up with him. In 1990 the Securities and Exchange Commission investigated Oracle for "pervasively inadequate accounting and billing practices." It was a complicated way of saying that the government thought that Larry

Ellison was a criminal. The investigation ended up costing the company $24 million. But the bad press was much worse. People began to doubt Oracle's honesty. The stock prices plummeted, and Ellison personally lost more than $3 billion.

But as he had in the past, Ellison simply refused to fail. He turned the company's image around—improving its customer support, halting the sale of "vaporware" (at least temporarily), and generally apologizing for being careless. And the public responded. Sales once again doubled. Oracle did a billion dollars' worth of business in 1993; in 1994 it grew to $2 billion . . . and by 1998 a whopping $7 billion. Ellison's personal net worth soared to $11 billion. There was no doubt about it: Oracle had conquered the relational-database market.

The Network Computer

Ellison wanted more, though. He *always* wants more—it is the defining feature of his personality. And in 1995 he believed he had finally found a way to beat Bill Gates. On Labor Day of that year he announced at a computer conference in Paris that the personal computer was a "ridiculous device." It was too old-fashioned, too complicated—what with its disk drives and hardware (he called it "bloatware") and constant need for upgrades. Just as minicomputers had replaced mainframes and PCs had replaced minicomputers, the time had come for something to replace the PC.

So Ellison proposed a "network computer" (NC). It was a radical new idea. The NC required no "bloatware" other than a screen, a keyboard, a printer, and a small box you could hook up to the Internet. Therefore, it would be a lot cheaper than a PC. About half the price, in fact. A web-based network would handle everything for you: software applications, personal files, games. It would be like a massive digital filing cabinet with limitless memory. Oracle would create this network, of course. Oracle would run it and maintain it and would also upgrade it for you. You would never need to buy software or new hardware again.

Theoretically, the system sounded amazing. Fast. Huge. Invisible. No more hassles. The NC did not exist yet, of course. But as always, Ellison talked first and worried about creating the product later. He even went on *Oprah* and scoffed at PCs. "The TV, the phone, water, electricity—we don't see the complex network behind *them*," he told her.

Larry Ellison, proponent of the "network computer"

"You never have to 'back up' your phone or TV. . . .Using a PC is like me flying my jet or helicopter to the store." He boasted that by the year 2000, NCs would outsell PCs by a ratio of nine to one.

But it seemed that the rest of the world was not ready to follow his lead. Especially the people at Microsoft. Gates gleefully pointed out the idea's flaws. Who would want to store personal files on a big system that could be accessed by anyone? Who could be sure of their privacy? And what if the system crashed? Would not *everyone* lose *everything*? He later joked: "Larry's hype has expanded to fill his ego."

Gates has so far proved to be right. People simply have not been ready to give up their PCs. The year 2000 has come and gone, and nobody owns an NC. But Ellison refuses to give up. If this idea does not eventually work out, something else will. It always does.

Dreams Can Come True

In the meantime Ellison is content to explore his many interests and watch his personal wealth blossom. He is currently at work on building a new mansion, which he claims will be "the most authentic Japanese structure outside Japan." It will be complete with an indoor koi pond, a rock garden, several meditation chambers . . . and a $50,000 television set.

He is also building a new yacht—350 feet (107 meters) long that will be the biggest privately owned boat in the United States. Being number one continues to be Ellison's top prior-

One of Larry's yachts, the *Sayonara*, that he races in sailing regattas several times a year

ity. He competes in sailing regattas several times a year. If he wins, he likes to fly over his vanquished opponents in one of his many planes—just for kicks. It is not enough to win.

A Russian MiG fighter jet—a potential purchase for Ellison

People have to know you are a winner. Incidentally, he is also looking to buy a Soviet-made MiG fighter jet. If he succeeds, it will be another first. Nobody else in America owns his or her own MiG.

Ellison still hopes that his self-interest will benefit others, though. He wants to improve medicine and health care; he donates large sums to many charities . . . and he has a little-known dream of providing a computer for every kid in

America. "That would mean I changed the world," he explains. "It would say something about *me*. I do everything for my own happiness, but the best way to pursue happiness is to do something for others. It's this nasty little trick."

It is hard to think of anyone else who would describe making the world a better place as "a nasty little trick." But that just might be the secret to Larry Ellison's success—a gift for saying the outrageous or unexpected and somehow making it all come true.

sources and bibliography

Carroll, Paul. *Big Blues: The Unmaking of IBM.* New York: Crown, 1993.

Dillon, Pat. *The Last Best Thing: A Classic Tale of Greed, Deception, and Mayhem in Silicon Valley.* New York: Simon & Schuster, 1996.

Dinerstein, Nelson T. *Database File Management Systems for the Microcomputer.* Glenview, IL: Scott, Foresman, 1985.

Kaplan, David. *The Silicon Boys and Their Valley of Dreams.* New York: HarperCollins, 2000.

Kaplan, Jerry. *A Silicon Valley Adventure.* Boston: Houghton Mifflin, 1995.

Riordan, Michael, and Lillian Hoddeson. *Crystal Fire: The Birth of the Information Age.* New York: Norton, 1997.

Wallace, James. *Overdrive: Bill Gates and the Race to Control Cyberspace.* New York: Wiley, 1997.

Wilson, Mike. *The Difference Between God and Larry Ellison: God Doesn't Think He's Larry Ellison.* New York: Morrow, 1997.

The following magazines and online services were also used:

Forbes

Fortune

Newsweek

PC Magazine

Time

Wired

www.cnnfn.com

www.nytimes.com

www.oracle.com

www.si.edu.com

Photography credits

AP/Wide World Photos, 8, 19, 25, 31, 33, 39, 70, 73, 75, 76
PictureQuest, 13

index

Page numbers in *italics* refer to illustrations.